A PLAYER'S WORLD MANUAL WANNA BE A PIMP

Ivory Wilson
First Edition, complete

PLAYERS WORLD

Ivory Wilson Self Publisher Washington DC 20001

PLAYERS WORLD

WARNING

If you're happy with your life the way it is now, don't read this book. I wrote this book thinking, that I might save a lot of young men from making the mistake I made. In this world that we live, it's man and woman. Once I became a pimp, I had lost the ability to feel or love most things in my life. I'll never get it again. That was my incense before I walk through that door of the Flamingo Club.

PLAYERS WORLD

Wanna Be a Pimp
The manual
By Ivory Wilson

A Players' world Enterprises
Post Office Box 70771
Washington, DC 20024 U.S.A.
playersworldenterprise@yahoo.com

All rights reserved. No part of this book may be reproduced or transmitted in any form or by any means without author's permission except for the inclusion of brief duration in a review.

PLAYERS WORLD

Copyright © 2012 by: Ivory Wilson
All rights reserved.

ISBN: 0-9744-8300-1
ISBN-13: 9780974483009

PLAYERS WORLD

About the Author

Ivory Wilson spent 20 years pimping whores across country. He went to sidewalk U, where most students were pimps, whores, drug dealers and murderers. He graduated at the head of his class, as a Blue Ribbon nigger, a pimp and a crook, capital P.I.M.P, pimp. Everywhere I go getting dough, players would walk up and ask pretty Red give me some game. Players' say game is to be sold, not told. That's why I am selling it to pimp and whores.

PLAYERS WORLD

Table of Contents

Chapter One
A players' World

Chapter Two
Things you need to see

Chapter Three
Wanna be a pimp?

PLAYERS WORLD

Chapter 1

PLAYERS WORLD 2000
Ivory Wilson

In the '70s, I was stationed on Custer Hill at Fort Riley, Junction City, and Kansas. Fort Riley was the largest army post in the Midwest. The first day I got there, my company commander told us "Don't go down town by yourself because you will meet a whore, and she will trick you in the alley, and her pimp will kill you for your money," As he was talking, I was thinking, " A pimp...I never seen a pimp before. Didn't know who that was. Every night we would go to the EM club and play pool. I got real good playing'. I was playing' so good, friends wanted me to go down town, at night, and hustle pool so I would meet this pimp named Sam. I said to myself, "that's that word again, pimp." I wanted to see a pimp now. I didn't want to get involved...just see one.

PLAYERS WORLD

My army friends would go downtown every night, but not me. I would stay in the barracks and play pool. They would always come back to the barracks and tell wild stories about pimps and whores.

The weekend was coming up and I had been on post 12 months. One Friday night, my army friends asked me to go with them downtown. I had never been downtown, so finally, I said "ok." My friend Mixon told me his home was in Florida. I like Mixon… he was the coolest nigger I had ever seen. He told me he was a player. Since I was a cowboy, I didn't know what a player was. We got in a cab, three in the front and three in the back. When we got in the cab, the driver asked, "you Cats going on the whore stroll?" Mixon said, "Yeah." We got downtown and Mixon told me to stay with him. The cab turned the corner on 10th Street and I had never seen anything like it before! There were whores everywhere you looked on both sides of the streets! The sidewalks were filled with soldiers, a café and mini motels. When the cab stopped, a whore walked up and got on top of the hood of the cab. She raised her dress up, with nothing on, and the guys in the cab

PLAYERS WORLD

went wild! The cab driver just laughed and said, "that crazy bitch!' I had never seen a pussy before.

While we were walking to a club called Flamingo, a whore ran up to me and put her hand on my dick and stuck her tongue in my ear. My wallet almost jumped out of my pocket! Mixon said, "Man, I don't date" and we walked into a dark red room with two pool tables in the corner of the room. There was one table and two chairs. There was a man in a three-piece suit. His hair was permed. He said to me, "Mixon is saying' you're a pool-shooting motherfucker. I'm going to find out!" Then the waitress came in, and he said, "Bring me a Hennessy on the Rocks." Then he said to me, "What are you drinking' Player?" Before I could answer, he told the waitress, "Bring two" and smiled at me. I realized this was Sam, the pimp!

Mixon didn't say anything. I looked at him to say something, but I was thinking, "When we're back on post, Mixon says he's a player all the niggers on post say they're players. I remember sometimes my Daddy and uncle would say they were players..." But then my thoughts were

PLAYERS WORLD

interrupted. Sam said, "Rack the ball, Pretty Red!" He turned and put something on the table. Mixon said, "Wilson, I will be in front of the club if you need me." "Ok," I said, "man, don't leave me!" I had never been around anything like this in my life. I'm thinking, "Who are these people? What is this place?" When I finished racking the balls, Sam said, "Come and get a toot." He picked up a card. At first I couldn't see what he was doing. I knew he was sniffing a white powder. It looked like an aspirin called "B.C. Powder" for headaches back home. I had never seen anyone do it like that before. He knew I had never seen coke before, or done it. He said "Come on Playa', it's on me. This is pure cocaine!" I walked to the table saying to myself, "it can't be that bad. He's sniffing it." I didn't want him to think I was a square. I picked up the card. I scooped up some of the white powder and sniffed it like I had seen him do. I didn't do it right because when I turned around he said, "Wipe your nose Pretty Red."

At first I didn't feel a thing. The waitress had both the drinks. I had never drank before either. I picked up the drink and drank some of it. It burned me. He laughed and said, "Sip it, it will go down easier." He

PLAYERS WORLD

broke the balls. A couple fell. When he was shooting, a woman walked in the room. He walked up to her and hit her with his pool stick. That shit happened so fast, I wasn't expecting anything like that to happen. She fell. I was raised a man don't fight women, but something inside me said, "mind your own business." The noise had a couple of people come to the door. The girl was getting up. The bartender came to the door, looked in, and said, "All shit, that's just Sam pimping'" She walked out in pain. He looked at me and said, "Man, I just took that punk bitch shopping. That bitch is going to need a doctor, if she don't have some money!" Then he asked, "Where you from Red?" I said, "Texas, I was riding' bulls in rodeos." He said, "Bulls, you crazy motherfucker! Texas! I've been there. It's not for me. There have been playing' niggers come from Texas. Me, Capital Pimp!" Music in the background, soft jazz. He was swaying back and forth smooth. He said, "Get another toot Pretty Red while I run this table on you."

He started shooting balls. They were falling everywhere. I was thinking he might run the table. He missed and said, "That's going to

PLAYERS WORLD

be your only shot, don't fuck it up." I didn't when I stopped shooting, the game was over. He said, "Man, it's going to be a long night. Now let's play this next game for money." I said, "Damn, we forgot to make a bet " He laughed, "Oh yeah, I'm going to break you. How much it cost for a cab to take you back to post? I said, " I don't know." He said, "Well, when I break you, I'll send you back." I had to laugh because I felt that if he'd give me a shot, I wouldn't miss. He said, "$10.00 a lesson." I laughed. From sniffing that stuff, I was feeling mellow. I never felt like this before. He knew that shit had me. When I broke, not one ball fell. He shot and missed. He cried out, "Ain't this a bitch!" At that time, two other players stroll in. They were dressed sharp like Sam. One of them said, "Sam, who are you back here breaking." At that time, I started shooting. They stopped talking. Sam said, "This motherfucker is going to run the table because I was dropping them." The two players were saying to Sam, "That's a pool-shooting motherfucker!" When I stopped shooting, the game was over. "Got damn, Got damn," Same cried out, then said, "Red, Come to the table. The other players were sitting at the table. One of them pulled out some coke and put it on the table. He said, "Y'all take a break. Try

PLAYERS WORLD

this shit." Sam said, "Go on Pretty Red, and get a toot." I did this time. I did it right. One of the players asked, "Red, have you been playing pool long?' I said, "No, I just started." He laughed and said, "Sam in trouble Kip." They laughed.

I had seen Super fly, The Mack, movies before I came there. I never dreamed that I would meet people like this. They were telling stories bout pimps that were from the 40s, 50s, and 60s. Kip asked me, "How old are you?" I said, "17." He laughed and said, "Shit, shooting like that, you're going to get paid tonight, because if you break Sam you're gonna have to break me too." They laughed. Sam said, Pretty Red, this is Kip, and Tat. They from Denver. Them niggers pimping up there. They laughed. Sam said, "Pretty Red, break Kip for me." Kip jumped up from the table and said, "how much we playing' for?" Sam hollered out, "$50 a game!" I said to myself, "Hell no, I can't shoot for that kind of money." Kip racked the balls. Sam said, "Red, just shoot. If you lose, I'll pay it. If you win, we split. Get another toot" I said, "Ok," and got another toot. Tat said, "Kip, they're over here plotting on you." Kip asked, "Who Sam and Red?" He laughed and said,

PLAYERS WORLD

"They can go fuck themselves. I'm going to win this" At that time, whores were coming in and out of the room like it was a revolving door, bring them money. Sam just sitting at the table with his legs crossed, laughing and tooting coke, saying he was a pimp and a crook.

Tat said, "One of the spices of life is jumping in and out of Cadillacs, snorting grade A cocaine and pimping whores." They laughed. I was excited about what I was seeing and hearing. I didn't know that Sam was planning to take me under his wings and give me the pimp game. My mind was taking in what I was seeing. I was studying them. Tat said, "It's my turn Kip." "I got the next game, " Kip said. Some of my army buddies were in an out of the room. When they did, Sam would say, "Ain't no whores back here, just pimps." I was sitting at the table with three major league pimps, because them kind of niggers don't fuck with square niggers." I was thinking, "Why me, I don't know how to be slick." They were sitting around the table counting money, kicking it. I was thinking to myself, "These are some real pimps." I looked at those big diamond rings them niggers were wearing. I'm still thinking, "I am the only square in here." The club was packed with soldiers and

PLAYERS WORLD

whores. Sam said, "Red, sit by me." I was still sipping that drink. The bartender came back and asked, "Is everything ok? Man, give me a toot!" Sam said, "It's on the table. Fast Teddy, this is Pretty Red, a pool-playing motherfucker. With the right schooling, he's going to be a pimp." Teddy said, "That's right. I know Sam getting money." They laughed. Ted continued, "Shit, Sam is macking for his." He looked at me and said, "Red, you are with some top-notch niggers here." Then he left. Tat said, "Yeah young light-skin nigger. I have seen the way them whores looking at you. Sam, we're going to turn some corners so I can check my traps." They both shook my hand. That's when I saw these niggers wore sharp like Mexican bandits.

Then strolled out. Sam, counting money, said, " I see you Red, you taking in this street life. I can see it in your eyes. You don't have too come from a big city to be a pimp. Me, my home is Memphis. Red, I travel cross-country pimping whores. It's a great world out there for a young pimp. I've met lots of niggers out here. Motherfuckers from everywhere. Comes here acting slick…can't stick they fingers in their asses. Red, you're a thinker. A pimp thinks. When I check that bitch

PLAYERS WORLD

you kept on shooting pool." He laughed as the drinks kept rolling in. I still had a drink that I hadn't touched. Mixon came in when he saw me kicking it at the table with Sam. He stopped at the pool table and asked, "Wilson, can I talk to you?" I got up and went over there. He said all excited, "man, you're in. That nigger is an international pimp!" I said, "Ok." He left. When I sat down, Sam said, "Man, do you believe that if you hang with a person everyday, it will rub off on you?" I said, "Yeah." He said, "I notice you just watching and listening. It's something about you. I know there is player in you. Tomorrow night, I want you to meet me here. Come along. That money you won, keep it. I'll win it from you one night. I've got to turn some corners. A bitch out there might want to choose a pimp. I have a story to tell you about a pimp and a whore. Tonight when you back on post, in your bed, ask yourself do you want to be a pimp? Your friends you have now, they won't be your friends if you turn into a real pimp. They can't accept "why you, not them." Square niggers act cool, they not sidewalk niggers. I know you want to tell your friend Mixon. He shoots dope, trick with whores. He's a fool. He's a cool nigger, not slick. He got fool in him, Red. If you put a fool in a room with an

PLAYERS WORLD

intelligent person for 30 days when you come back, you will find two fools. You can't teach a fool shit. Pretty Red, toot that that coke that's left on the table." He strolled out. Soldiers were coming in now looking at me crazy. I didn't give a fuck.

Here comes Mixon saying, "Man, you got it going on! Man, let me have the coke!" I said, "you can have that drink," and with a scoop, I did it. He said, "That shit is hard to find here. The town is full of heroin. Niggers coming from Nam, that's all they, want and some pussy. Wilson, let's go up to the street to another club." I was feeling good too. Had won money. I said, "Ok." Walking out of the club, the bartender said, "I'll see you tomorrow Pretty Red." Mixon said, "Pretty Red them niggers like you. They gave you a pimp name. You got to tell me what he was telling you Man." The sidewalks were filled with soldiers and whores walking up the sidewalk. They were watching me. They were asking guys, "Hey baby, you want to go party? Wanda goes have some fun? Pussy for sale or rent." One was heading for me when another whore grabbed her arm and whispered something into her ear. She smiled and said, "Hi Red." They would

PLAYERS WORLD

not come close to me. They did when I got out that cab. I said to myself, "What happened." I was looking all around. It looked like Hollywood was there making a pimp movie. Pimps were standing on the sidewalks. The track was only two blocks long. It looked like they were having a fashion show.

When we passed them, from being in that club with Sam, all the players spoke. Walking to the next club Mixon kept on asking what we were talking about. I told him to wait, I would tell them later. I wasn't going to tell. I was told not to and I wasn't going to. We walked in the club. It was dead, just a few people. Around the corner the track life was jumping. I looked at the bar. There were two girls. Mixon said, "I know one of them. I'm going to rap to them. He came back with them. Sitting at the table, Mixon said, "What are y'all drinking?" One of the girls said "Vodka and orange juice." The others said a beer. I said I had enough drinks. One of the girls said, "We know, we saw you early at the Flamingo Club, at the table with pimps." One of them said, "You can't talk? My name is Kitty and this is Pat. Red, when are you going to teach me to play pool?" I said, "Now". There were a few balls

PLAYERS WORLD

left from someone's game. She asked, "Do you have a girlfriend?" I said, "No." She bent over the pool table, with her ass in my face. She said, "Help me with this shot. I can't make it." So I put my arms around her, my dick got rock hard. She wiggled a couple of times. "How long have you been on post," she asked. "I just got here from Texas," I answered. A slow song was playing. She slowly said, "Let's dance Red." She got me on that floor, got to grinding on my dick, nibbling on my neck, saying, "I like you. A fine looking red man." I was looking around and saw a pimp with his back to me.

I could not see who it was. She said, "Red, it's getting late. Would you walk me home? The club will close soon. I don't live far and you can call a cab from my house. Thinking with my dick, I told Mixon I was leaving with her. He replied, "Ok Wilson, I know you can handle yourself, I saw that tonight." Walking out the door, someone said, "Hey Sugar Dick." I looked and it was Sam. He kept walking pass us. She said, " You know him?" We stopped at the door, looking out. I saw this super fly caddie parked in front. I said, "Damn, that a bad motherfucker there!" She goes, "Huh, that your pimp friend's car.

PLAYERS WORLD

You need to stay away from him; he's a bad man. Red, he has 10 girls working the street for him. He's at least 60." I didn't answer her. She continued, "He's a gangster pimp. He beat up a girl friend. She was so scared, she left town. I don't want you to hang with him." I kept looking at that car. Walking her home, we came to a small park. She said, "let's stop here Red for a moment," We started kissing on the bench. She stood up and dropped her panties. When I saw that wet willie for the first time, I busted a nut before I could get it in. She laughed saying, "That's all right Red," and put her titty in my mouth. We were on top of the bench. I try to act like I knew what to do. She knew I didn't know we were on the table fucking like two minks. When we got to her house, she gave me her phone number. Everyone in the house was asleep. She went into a back room and said, "Come here Red. Sit here." She unsnapped my pants and sat on my dick again, saying, "I want to see you again Red. Say you will come back." When I got back on post, the sun was coming up. Good thing it was Saturday because I was a top soldier. Spit, shine boots, starch fatigues everyday. I lay in my bed thinking of that pimp life. I saw myself driving a freak off caddie of my own. My head was spinning. It was

PLAYERS WORLD

saying to me "Pimp Red, money, girls, suits, rings, fly caddie." I could not get those thoughts out of my head. I could not sleep.

At noon I went to the mess hall. Most of the cats were there eating. A cat from a company I didn't know, but had seen around, said, "I seen you last night kicking it with them pimps. Them niggers down with the game. I hustle pool too…Push a little weed." As he was talking, I was eating. A couple of cats from "C" company, my company, sat down saying, "Wilson, man, them niggers you were with, they got the town lock down for years, Bro!" All them cool army niggers were into that black shit. Bro this, and bro that. They would kill me with that shit. Everyone wanted me to talk about last night. I wanted to, but I remembered Sam had said don't, so I didn't. I told them I had met Kitty. One of the cats said, "I know her. She was fucking Dennis…the cat that was shipped out for Germany." I didn't say anything. I just looked at him. I was leaving when Mixon walked up with a cool nigger named Jet from New York Mixon said, "Wilson, man let's go to the E.M club. It's still pay day." I was still worn out from last night. Every motherfucker I met was a player. At first, I thought they all were

Dispatch Note

Order Number 103-2545029-5022638

Supplied by PaperbackshopUS

Catalogue Number	Title and Artist	Qty
9780974483009	A Player's World Manual: Wanna Be A Pimp? [Paperba	1

Thanks for shopping with us. Please note that if you ordered more than one item we may ship them in separate packets. If you have a query about your order please email us at:

pbshopus@paperbackshop.co.uk

Returns: Please enclose this slip with your items and return to the address on the front of the packet.
Why are you returning the item? _____
Would you prefer a refund or a replacement? _____

Please note, with some items a replacement is not possible.

PLAYERS WORLD

until last night. When it was my turn to play, they came around the table, talking loud, trying to be seen. When I finished playing pool that afternoon, I had won $80 off them. Mixon and other niggers were in the corner with Jet, drinking, singing, dancing and partying. Jet asked, "Wilson, what time you going downtown? We can roll together." Now this was a cool nigger like bro Mike from Philly. They were dealing drugs on post. I said, "If I go downtown, it will be in cab,"

It's Saturday night. I hit the track. Fast Teddy told me that Sam had bumped an associate, and was rolling now I was going to the track every night rolling with other players. Each one served me some game about pimping whores. Games from Memphis, New York, Denver, Texas, LA, Kansas City, MO, Detroit, and Oklahoma. I was jumping in and out of caddies every night. I had formed a jigsaw puzzle in my mind. A lot of spaces were empty as I was seeing the game being played. They were filling in fast. I was gambling, shooting dice, playing poker, dealing dope, stacking paper, still creeping over to Kitty's house. By now, I had met the family, but not telling the players. I knew they would roast me for that. Six weeks later, Sam

PLAYERS WORLD

was back in town. Rolling with Sam, he said, "I saw you with that punk bitch. That bitch is a player. This is a wild ass army town, with over 75 unsolved murders. Them fool ass soldiers, coming from the war. Come down here thinking they can beat a bitch up, take her money and get away. They fuck up and get smoked. That bitch is a local. She comes out and catch a soldier on pay day nights. She tried to work the track, but don't want to pay a pimp. A bitch must have a pimp or she can't work. If you see a bitch working, go and asked her does she have man? If she say no, she don't need one. Say you must choose me or some other player before the night is over. Then walk away. Let the other players know that an outlaw bitch is working without a man. They will spit at her if I know one gets any action from her. We will wait for her coming from turning a trick and kick her ass and take her money. She will choose someone or leave town. Red, on your turf, when you bump, go to him strapped with that bitch. Serve him and put that bitch back to work. When a pimp's whore is giving you action, eyeballing and smiling, say something to her. You can read what's on a bitch's mind. A pimp catches, whores bump him. Pimps are not friends with each other, only associates. If my bitch gives you

PLAYERS WORLD

action, bump me, because if your bitch gives me action, I will bump you. If your game is tight, we will become close associates and ride to different cities and bump other niggers. Try not to catch a nigger's only bitch. You may have to smoke him." I ask why. He continued, "Because she is all that he have. Car note, rent bills. If he's been having her, only her, they are not a pimp and whore; they are husband and wife team. If you do, call him while rolling with her.

Chapter 2

Things You Need to Know

"Red, it's something you need to see." He drove around the corner and stopped in front of a whorehouse. He said, "When we go in here, an old pimp named Bill own the joint. And that there are trick's rooms in there in the back; Bill has holes cut in the rooms. Whores don't know. So pimps can see if his bitches is stuffing his money from him when she get from a trick." We walk into Bill's. There were six whores sitting at a table with five soldiers having a drink. One of the soldier

PLAYERS WORLD

had some big-rimmed eyeglasses on We walk pass them going into the back. Bill was sitting at a table counting money with his pistol on the table. He said, "Pimping Sam, who is this." Sam replied, "This is Pretty Red." Bill, leaning out of his chair to get a better look said, "Oh yeah, that red nigger is pretty. Nigger, if you ever bump me, you better ride with her." We laughed. Sam said, "Red, when one of my bitches, go in look, I did. They walked in. She asked him for her money. He gave it to her. She said, "You only have 15 minutes," and put a towel on the bed. He took off all his clothes. She didn't. He asked her to take if off. She said, "Give me more money." He did. She laid on the towel. This nigger had a mule dick. He was going up in this bitch saying, "Oh, this pussy is so good. It's mine, don't you like this?" She said, "Oh yeah baby, your dick is so big and good. You are really fucking me." She pulled his face to her chest and looked at her watch and said, "Your time is up. Next."

She took a wet towel and wiped him off. They put their clothes on and came out. The second one came in with that soldier with the glasses on. He paid her and they got naked. She said, "Now, I don't want no

PLAYERS WORLD

shit out of you this time nigger." "What do you mean?" He said. "I mean when your time is up, it's up. Ok, I don't want any trouble." She got in the bed on her knees, with ass in his face. He put his left hand on her back and started sucking her ass and jacking off with his right hand. I said, "Bad Motherfucker. Sam you got to see this." We were laughing. He said, that's one of my money getting bitches, Red. Never put a bitch on a quota, a slick bitch with game. Knows you ask for $100 a night from her only. It's six workdays in a whore workweek. She will start turning tricks fast, sending money home and giving you only a $100 a night and get away with it. Make sure you're not far from your bitches when they're working. The town lets pimps work their whores here because of that big-ass army post. All them motherfucking soldiers. If there weren't any whores here, them fool-ass soldiers would be down here rapping them square bitches. This town will soon dry up when the war is over. There are lots of pimps here now. When you find a city with a lot of pimps and whores, they are getting money. If they wasn't, they wouldn't be there."

PLAYERS WORLD

"Dope is the only thing that sell faster than pussy. Out here, you do lots of things, but you can only be good at one. You can get a big bankroll dealing dope. Fast catch a bitch, stop dealing." It was almost sun up. Sam continued, "Red, I can't bring you on post, but I can drop you so you can catch a cab." He pulled over. "Here you drive Pretty Red." I sat in that driver seat, driving that UFO on wheels. I went back on post. The next night, I called Kitty. She said, "Red, I'm pregnant." I said, "What! Are you sure?" She said, "Yes, I need to see you. Are you coming over?" I said, "Yeah, I'll be there." I was in my room getting dressed when Dixon walked in. I said, "Man, Kitty is pregnant." Mixon said, Wilson, Kitty was seeing a guy that shipped out just when you hat here. She is pregnant for him, that's why he got a transfer out. Wilson, you my dog. I wouldn't fuck with you like that. Check it out Man." I was hurt. I went to her house. All I could see in my mind was Sam, face smiling saying, "Hey Sugar dick." I asked her, "Do you know a guy name Dennis?" She said, "No, why, yeah, What for." Tears were rolling down her face. "I'm sorry Red, I lie. It's not your baby, but I love you. We can make it work." I walked away. I

PLAYERS WORLD

stopped in the park, and sat on that bench. My thoughts were of being played like Trick Tracy.

I could feel my heart hardening. My thoughts changing. I walked to the track and told them what happened. Sam smiled and said; "Now you have a pimping license Pretty Red." Sitting at the table were two pimps from Kansas City, Mo. They were brothers. They asked, "Red, ride with us to Kansas City. You might bump. Some of them niggers up there are not pimping, they are sugaring." I left, rolling with the twins. My mind had blocked out the fact that I was still a soldier. They both had big stables. They were saying, "Red, when you hit the track, put your work in. Get on them niggers' bitches. Two pimps rolling together can catch, not three. Dave is going to stay in tonight. Me and you will turn some corners and patrol the track." First we went shopping. I invested in myself. I bought two pimp hats, five different colored suits, shirts, ties, scarves to match, and five pairs of shoes. When we got to the condo, I went to my room and tried on my suits. Getting suited up and strapped up.

PLAYERS WORLD

The track, 12th St and Main. Pimp niggers riding pretty. When I saw all those different color flavored whores, I got excited. I was acting like a kid in a candy store. A voice in my head said, "It's Showtime Red. Get down for your cookies and grits. Pimp or die." We started turning corners. I was riding shotgun. When we rolled up to whores working, Fred would slow down so I could spit at them. The first couple of hours, nothing. Pimp niggers riding too, watching their whores now. Fred stopped at a club so we could get a drink. A couple of pimps rolled up and said, "Pimping Fred, you still getting money out of that wild ass army town. Fred said, "None, stop. Larry, Gerald, this Pretty red." They spoke and said they were going north soon and that Ron is getting paid in Chicago.

Gerald said, "Twin we're going to turn some corners. Y'all are safe." When they rolled out, Fred said, "Red, you got them niggers nervous. Stay on them niggers' whores. Somebody might get bumped." Every time we would turn a corner, they would be turning. I said, "Man, fuck this." I got out. Smelling sweet, mixing with them niggers' whores, making sure I short stopped everyone of them that I caught eyeballing

PLAYERS WORLD

me. Asking them for a light, what time is it...just to stop her so she can see me. Getting back to the car before the other niggers rolled around again. Walking pass a group of whores, one of them said to the others, "Girls, he is full of catch action." I heard that and stopped and turned around. I said, "I would like to talk to you when you're not working." She replied, "I'm not working now. What is your name?" I said, "Pretty red." She smiled and said I liked it. She said, "My name is Sandy." I said, "Let's go into the alley so we can talk. It won't be long before your man will be looking for you. So give me that money because if he catches us, he will beat on you. If you don't show me that you mean well, I can't protect you." She reached in her bra and gave me that dough. I asked, "What is your man's name?" "Stick Man, from Minnesota. They just got here," she said, "Give me 30 minutes. Pick me up here." I turned the corner and stopped Fred. I got in the car and went in my pocket and pulled out them pimp dollars. Fred asked, "Get any action." I said, "Got that whore, got that dough, we got to go!"

PLAYERS WORLD

Fred said, "What! You whore-catching motherfucker!" He was laughing. "Red, that's right, Pimp Red, who is her man?" I said, "Stick Man from Minnesota. She said they been here a week." Now we're rolling the track, looking to see him so when I pick up that bitch, I'm going to serve him. Rolling on Main Street and Armour Street to a club called Mr. Bibbs. All them pimp niggers parked while their bitches working. We saw the Minnesota license tag on a caddie. We rolled and picked up this jazzy white bitch. She got in the car. I knew that my name wasn't Prince Charles, but he wasn't going to live better than me. We rolled up to the club. She asked, "What if he don't give you my clothes?" I said, "If he don't we'll get new ones." We walked in the club and left her in the car. We walked to the players, table pimp niggers, popping it like it goes, down and dirty. Larry and Gerald were sitting at the table. When they saw us, they knew somebody had been knocked. The look in their faces. They thought it was one of their whores. They go quiet. I asked, "Which one of you players name Stick Man?" That nigger looked at me. He had been sitting at the club talking slick to the nigggers about he's an international pimp and can't be bumped. That nigger stopped talking. I said, "Your bitch has

PLAYERS WORLD

chosen." He crumbled like a cookie when I told him I had knocked him. He said, I need to hear that from her." We walked outside. He was trying to tell me that she owed money. He was going to burn her clothes. I said, "Stick, I got that whore and that dough. You can have them clothes. We got to go." He asked, "Can I talk with her alone?" I said, "No." He asked her, "Did you chose him?" She said, "Yes."

Fred and Gerald were walking behind us a few feet away. If we were in Minnesota, I would have rolled out with her. He didn't have a choice but to accept getting bumped. Anything else would have been like throwing bricks at a shoot-out. He walked over to Gerald and Fred. Gerald and Stick Man walk back to the club. Fred walked over and said, "Red, motherfuckers didn't know you when you got here. They know you now." I put that bitch back to work. The next day, I put that bitch on a bus so she can cross the state line. I picked her up after she crossed over. We hit the track in "anything goes" Junction City. I put my game down and strolled in the club. Sam, sitting at a table smiling, said, "I knew you were a pimp, Red." Sam and Fast Teddy were in the back gambling, shooting dice and breaking some

PLAYERS WORLD

tricks. A few guys from my company were also there. My bitch came in and gave me that dough. Twenty-four hours later, the word had got back on post that Wilson is back in town pimping. The M.P. was there to take me away. I knew it was going to happen. Now I'm sitting in a dark cell and my whore downtown. I'm thinking how my life has changed so fast. I knew I was going to get bumped. The next day, my company commander came to see me and said, "PFC Wilson, it has gotten back to me that you have been gambling, dealing dope and running with pimps. You are a soldier, not a fucking pimp. You will be sent to a retraining brigade. I said, "What, hell no. I want out, fuck the army!"

He left. Sitting in the stockade, no word from the track. My bitch in a hotel room. I could feel the game had chosen me. A week later, Mixon came to see me and said, "Fred have your clothes and you have been bumped. Wilson, what bump mean?" I told him that is pimp talk. I was thinking, "Damn, I got bumped by Fred. Mixon asked, "Wilson, how long will you be in here? Man, is there anything I can do for you. I can go downtown and watch your whore." I had to laugh. I don't

PLAYERS WORLD

have a whore, I've been bumped. I knew the only reason I got bumped was because I wasn't there to be on that bitch's ass. I said, "Thanks Man, but no." He said, Wilson, you have changed. You're a player. Wilson, give me some game." I said, "Man, one day we will talk about it." He left. Two months passed and I'm still locked down. My platoon sergeant came to see me and asked, "Wilson, you were a good soldier, expert rifleman, a bull rider...Why are you throwing it all away to be a pimp. That street life is going to lead you to prison or death." The army has decided to discharge you." He left. I knew if I went back home they would be glad to see me. My mother would have made me breakfast in bed for a couple of days. On that third day, there would be a newspaper folded by my breakfast with circles around jobs. No, I was not going home being a failure.

I turned 18. Locked down. Eight days later my platoon sergeant and CO came back. They brought a lot of papers for me to sign. When I finished signing them, my CO said, "You are discharged from the Army." I called a cab to take me downtown. Going downtown in the cab, I was throwing my army clothes out the window. On the track,

PLAYERS WORLD

Sam was sitting in his same spot, counting money. "Whore, Pimping Red, them motherfuckers let you out?" "Yeah," I said, "I got a discharge." "Red, you got bumped." "I know. Mixon came to see me. Fred bumped me?" "No, Fred didn't bump you. A nigger from Los Angeles bumped you and rolled out with her. She left your clothes with Fred." Laughing, he said, "Oh yeah, that nigger said to tell you he got that whore, and dough, and had to go." We laughed. "Red, your game is tight. Niggers had been spitting at her every night. She didn't give anybody any action for a week. She didn't know if you would ever get out." I took the pimp game and ran with it. I had diamonds put in my teeth, a big diamond ring on each pinkie finger. Every time I spoke to a bitch, I caught one. I kept a pocket of kryptonite. It wasn't long before I had two whores, and punk in a trunk, with a ski mask on slanging.

PLAYERS WORLD

Chapter 3

WANNA BE A PIMP

If you believe that anything is possible, just because you've never seen it, doesn't mean the pimp game don't exist. The pimp is not dead. It's the niggers that know the game that are dead or in prison. The pimp game is not meant for every man. Some players get it from a spoon. A pimp gets is from bitches' wounds. If a bitch didn't have a wound, she would be running through the woods with a bounty on her head. In every city, there are whores and strolls. Before you can become a blue-ribbon nigger with a PH.D in pimping whores, you must first have knowledge about the pimp life. Without the knowledge, you can't pimp no bitch. It's good to learn about pimping when you're a young man. At night, the tracks come alive. If you have pimp in you, you will feel it when you see it being played. Some players will tell you truth and fiction, but if you're a real player, you will get it. Ask yourself when you're alone, "Is this the life I really want?" because

PLAYERS WORLD

you will have to make some changes in your life. Your friends and family will change. They won't understand you once you become a pimp.

The only person that likes a pimp is a bitch. You got to get exposed to the game first before you can spit at her about whoring for you. A flashy car, a big bank roll, suits, and rings won't make you a pimp without the knowledge first about pimping whores. You must learn to study bitches' minds, look them in the eyes and con them into whoring for you. Bitches choose pimps for different reasons. She may like the way you walk and talk. So, it you're on the job sites every night, what goes around will come around again for you. Remember, one of the spices of life is jumping in and out of Cadillacs and pimping whores. She won't volunteer, but she will if you trick her. She may not in her hometown, because she was raised there. Her friends and family will see and hear that she is whoring for you. It won't work. You must take her to another track in another city. Get her a fake ID, under a new name that she likes and that bitch will pay you.

PLAYERS WORLD

A pimp is not a gangster. A pimp is in a class of his own. A pimp can act like a gangster if you fuck with his dough or his hoe. You will think he's Al Capone. A pimp has vision. He sees the obstacles that are stacked against him. He sees where he is heading in this sporting life ten or twenty years from now. A big bank roll, savings accounts, investments. That he must have when it's all over. You can be in the pimp game ten or twenty years and come out with nothing for all those years that you've been a sidewalk nigger, if you don't save that dough. Being a pimp is a lonely life. You will learn to deal with society or you'll be dead or in prison. All your thoughts must be kept secret. Pimps don't do anything for a bitch unless it's his idea first. A pimp has logic about pimping whores.

Most bitches, like sex, fantasize about men's different dick sizes. A pimp use his wits and gives a bitch some direction on how she can get paid and have fun fucking. A good pimp gets her to see the difference between fucking and not getting paid. When the feeling is gone, reality slaps her in the face. Bills and rent will be there when she finishes nutting. A pimp knows that a bitch will work if he is a man and stays

PLAYERS WORLD

true to the game. A pimp only fucks whores on Sundays because that's the only day she has off. I was told it was sin to pimp whores on Sundays, so I started giving them Sundays off. You see, when a bitch is working the tracks, turning six or seven tricks a night, she is fucking and sucking dicks longer and sorter than yours, so when she comes in at night, she is tired. Now, here you come wanting to fuck her. If you start fucking her every night, telling her that her pussy is sunshine, she hears that from tricks, she will soon form an opinion about you. Her opinion of you is that you're not a pimp; you're a sugar dick.

You can't pimp no bitch if you think with your dick. You can't pimp no bitch that you're in love with. If you can control a bitch's mind, you will automatically have her body. A pimp makes sacrifices. He does things that he doesn't want to do, but he must to survive. The reward at the end of the rainbow is what he wants. A pimp is an actor, a bitch is an actress. It's king and Queen, but King comes first. I became a major league whore pimp, not by nature, only by profession. Before you can put a bitch on the track, you must school her about pimp life. In order to be a good pimp, you must realize that every woman is not

PLAYERS WORLD

meant to be a whore. A smart pimp can talk to any bitch for ten minutes and know if she will fit in his plans. If she doesn't, she won't see him again. A smart pimp knows that for every woman that won't whore for him, there is a bitch that will. Don't let a bitch tell you she won't whore, but she likes you. Tell her if you can get a dollar from every bitch that tells you she likes you, you would be rich.

You can't have square bitches on the side and bitches whoring for you. If your whores find out that you're "free fucking", and spend their money on square bitches, they will choose another pimp. You have blown it. If that happens, charge it to the game. It's true that almost every black man has thought of pimping once in his life. Once you become a pimp and a crook, you will have to play them bitches because a bitch is a player. She will study you. Bitches learn the game from pimps too. She chose you to be her pimp, then be pimp and get paid. Once you show a bitch a big bankroll, don't show her anymore. You can call her bitch and whore because money is power. Let her find out that an elephant has stepped on your bankroll and the money is gone, you can't call her bitch or whore. If you do, she will make you wish

PLAYERS WORLD

that you never caught her. The same things that make you laugh, will also make you cry. A woman comes for her man, not because he has a big dick. What makes a woman come is how she feels about you. Once you have bitches selling pussy for you, don't be ashamed of what you have become. If you do, don't be in it.

Pimping is like anything else in life. If you don't put anything in it, you won't get anything out of it. You must be dedicated, in your walk and your talk. You must look like a pimp, dress like a pimp, and smell like a pimp at all times. Pimps come from the south. Gangsters come from the east and gamblers come from the west. Coming up in the pimping game, a young Mack should not try to catch a seasoned bitch. It's best to start with a bitch that you can mold into the way you want her to pay you. The pimp game won't work for you if you try to pimp a bitch that know you before you became a pimp. You must start fresh. That seasoned bitch has a track record. She has been with a few pimps. She will know that you're not a seasoned pimp, and she will comb your head for that statement. She will play you like a Virginia vilain, smoother than a motherfucker.

PLAYERS WORLD

Once you understand the pimp game and how it's played, go out and meet a square white bitch. A white bitch is easy to flip. They love adventure. A black man's world is exciting to her. She will accept other bitches easier into your stable. A black bitch won't. You can have two snow bunnies, and one black. The black bitch will run them off. Why you ask? Because if you're on the floor having some pimp fun, ringing your nuts out, and the black one is waiting her turn, what do you think is going through her mind? "Look at the black-ass nigger with them two white bitches. They should be up her watching us!" She will do everything she can to run them off, and then leave you. Don't mix salt and pepper. It won't last for long.

When you meet a young bitch that likes you because you're a sidewalk nigger, she will ask you what do you do for a living. Tell her you're a gambler. A gambler takes chances. Take her out to dinner and pull out your bankroll. Have at least $2,500 in cash. No dough, no whore, after dinner, take her some place where y'all can sit and talk alone. Pull out your roll and ask her to count it for you. Before you put your bankroll

PLAYERS WORLD

in this bitch's hand, make sure you have counted it first. Remember a bitch is a player. Most bitches have never seen that much at one time. When she is counting that dough, look her in the eyes. This is your job to study her. You will see what she sees and what she is thinking. When she is counting that dough, she sees shoes, dresses, jewels, and a car. After she has counted it and gives it back, take out your pistol sitting it on the table and recount your roll. Make sure it's right. If it's short, check that bitch. Put your hands on her. Smack her and say it's not you. It's those demons and devils that are locked inside you. If the dough is right when she gives it back to you, ask her if she likes excitement and adventure. If she says yes, tell her that you're the nigger she should be fucking with. Look her in the eyes and say that you have plans to be rich, and if you had a bitch, you would be a pimp. Tell her that you're like Ford. You have an idea on how the game goes. Take her home, and don't call her. The next time she sees you she will know you keep a big bankroll. She will be all up on you like you have peppermint on your breath. Niggers will be asking, "Man, what did you do to her for her to be all up on you like that?" Don't wake the dead. A secret ain't a secret if you tell somebody. They can't control

PLAYERS WORLD

one bitch and here you come controlling five or more bitches. They won't like you for that. Stay away from cool niggers.

Feelings are one of the strongest forces on this earth. So you know what you will do for a bitch anything she asks when you're in love with a bitch. Well, when a bitch is in love with a slick nigger, she will do the same. Don't tell her that you're in love with her. Pimps don't fall in love. He only loves what a bitch can do for him. When she's finished saying she's in love with you, call an associate and say she's ready. Have a pimp call you right back in ten minutes. Leave her in the room alone and go into the bathroom. Close the door, run your bath, and jack off. You'll last longer. When the phone rings, tell her to answer it. Remember, she just told you that she's in love with you. You've been telling her you're a gambler, not a pimp. When she answers the phone, the voice will say, "Man, the police got your whores and their money, and they're looking for you!" He will hang up. The bitch will be in shock, now that she knows you're a pimp and a crook, because you just stole her heart. Her feelings are strong for you. She can't walk away from you.

PLAYERS WORLD

Come out of the bathroom acting like you don't know what just happened. She will be crying and saying "You're a pimp, don't try to lie. Your friend just called and said the police got your whores and money." Say, "Ok, it's out now. I didn't want you to get hurt." Start getting your things together like you're leaving town. Give her cab fare. She will say she loves you and what about her. Tell her you care for her, but you must leave her because you're a pimp. She will say take her with you. Tell her she can't come because you're pimping whores. She will ask what does she have to do to be with you? Pull her close to you and say to yourself, "Hollywood couldn't catch these moves on film, but you're a playing motherfucker because you just caught a bitch."

Sit her down and pull out your bankroll. Pull out your pistol. Sit them on the table and say, "This money is for us. If you get picked up by the police, sit still, I will get you right out." You will send a bail bondsman. Tell her the police will say that they don't want her, they want her pimp. They will try to get her to sign a paper called "white

PLAYERS WORLD

slavery." If she signs it, you will get 10 years in prison. If you don't get her out, she will sign and go free. Put your hand on your pistol and say, for your freedom, if she signs anything, when you get out of prison, you will find her and kill her and her family. She will say she understands. Tell her about the track and about how you want her to get your money. Tell her if a pimp comes up to her o the track and asks if she's happy with you, to say "yes." A seasoned pimp will respect that and roll out. If he doesn't leave her alone, tell her to call you. When this situation happens, for your props, go to him strapped. Respect is everything. If a bitch doesn't respect you, she is not going to pay you. You may have to drape some dram. Make an example out of him and the rest will leave her alone.

If you don't handle your business, she won't be able to work the tracks nowhere. Some players say the game is cop and blow. I say the game is cop, lock and hold. A bitch won't mind working the streets or hotels if she knows you're there to protect her. Tell her don't let no bitch come up to her and say that she's got a trick that wants two girls. Don't go with her. She is trying to play her out of pocket. You will have to

PLAYERS WORLD

hang around her for a few days until she gets the hang of it. After she catches the game, you stay off the track, because you can be on the track every night, cleaner than a Safeway chicken and niggers will say you're just another clean nigger, but the police will know you. Their job is to catch you. Your job is for them not to. A slick nigger stays out of jail, not in. You can't be slick if you're locked up. Out of sight, out of mind.

Tell her don't leave the track unless she is going to turn a trick. Don't let her call you and say it's a slow night, or it's starting to rain. Tell her to walk between the raindrops, but get your money. The day you lay off is the day they pay off. Tell her don't let no one tell her you said nothing because you're a pimp, not Captain "Save a Whore". If you don't know, she sure doesn't know. She doesn't know any more than what you tell her. Tell her that when she meets a trick, ask to see his ID. If he doesn't show it, tell her to walk away from him. If he do show it, tell her to ask him if he is a police officer of any kind. If he says "No", and busts her, that is entrapment. You will beat it in court.

PLAYERS WORLD

Tell her when a trick asks her out much tell her not to quote a price. Let him quote prices. When he says the price she wants, stop him.

Start kissing her. Lay her on the bed. Ask her if she is going to be your bitch? She will say, "Yes". Just before you go up in her ask her is she going to pay you. She will say, "Yes". When you're finished ringing your nuts out, ask her will she go through some pain for you. She will say, "Yes". Roll her over and put your dick in her ass. Make her scream like a pig, "Wee, Wee". If you don't, a trick will. Remember, you can get a bitch out, but she can't get you out. Tell her don't get into the car with a trick. Have him meet her at the hotel. She will take a cab there. Tell her if she gets in his car, you can't protect her. Tell her don't stick her face in a trick's car window. He might snap and cut her face, then pull off. Tell her to stand back from his car. Get two hotel rooms, side by side. Don't sign for the rooms in your name. Get someone else to sign, not you. Keep nothing but rubbers in the room that she is working. The other is where you will sit with your pistol. When she is working, tricks will never know you're there unless he fucks up. Tell her if she has a situation with him, just knock on the

PLAYERS WORLD

wall. Tell her to just get the chain off the door and you will handle your business. Make sure that you keep both keys to the rooms. Tell her when she finishes turning a trick, let him leave the room first, then put your trap money in the drawer. You will get it when she goes back to the track.

$200 a day will change any motherfucker's lifestyle. Start getting more than that a day and see what happens. Sit in that room and pimp them bitches. Put that trap money in a shoebox for thirty days. Only pay for rooms and food. If you haven't been bumped in 30 days, you will have her locked down. Your game is tight. You're now running for Capitol Pimp. If you don't campaign, you don't get elected. The way you start out is the way you'll end up. The only limits you have are the ones you put on yourself. A pimp dresses for success so when you go out and campaign, act real pimpish. You will catch. A conversation rules the nation. Go on the tracks again, and when you see a bitch eyeballing you, look her in the eyes, grab your dick, walk up to her and ask if you can talk to her when she's not working. If she says, "No, I have a man", then reply "Ok, if not this year, maybe next year", then roll out.

PLAYERS WORLD

When a bitch tells you she has seen you on the track, but her friends have been saying you're a pimp. She wants to see if you will admit it. Say that I am bitch. If she stays and talks with you, you've just caught another bitch.

When you bring her home, your Main Bitch will blow up. Don't talk, just check that bitch. Put your hands on her. Put her outside and close the door. She won't leave. She has invested in you. Do this, and you will have two whores. If you don't do this, you'll have no whores. Two monies are better than one. If you don't do this, you're not a pimp, just a sugar dick. If you can't control one bitch, you sure can't control two. You must control one first. That new bitch will see what happened in your game. She chose you, not her. If you send her back to the track, she will tell the other whores and they will tell their pimps that you're not pimping, you're sugaring. So now, you're two deep and can't get any sleep. Keep your dick in your pants and bitches will pay you. Two players traveling together can look out for each other. Birds of a feather fly together.

PLAYERS WORLD

Now your pimp game is flawless. No two players see the game the same way. It's the caliber of the players. It's a solo game that only you can play. Manage that dough ad that whore won't leave you. So when you see a big Mack turning corner, don't get animosity, get inspired that you can be one too! Still want to be a pimp?

PLAYERS WORLD

A Players' World Enterprises
                      Book By Ivory Wilson
                      Book Return Policy

Our books are returnable if a title isn't moving in your market we want to get it back before, a new edition makes it obsolete. Thank you for giving it a chance on your valuable shelf space. Our return period is normally ninety days after one year, as long as the edition is still in print. To keep our product current we update our title every one and a half to two years.

Ship Books to A Players' World Enterprises
      P.O. Box 70771, Washington, DC 20024

        Book damaged in transit are not the responsibilities of the publisher. Please make claim to the carriers to package the books so that this will survive the trip.
             Do not use "diffy bags".

Post Office Box 70771   Washington, DC 20024 U.S, A (202) 276-5274

PLAYERS WORLD

We are pleased to be able to send you this Review copy and would appreciate receiving two copies of your review.

A Players' World Wanna be a Pimp, The manual
        By Ivory Wilson

>   Publication Date: July 1, 2004

- ❖ $55.00 Trade paper back
- ❖ $110.00 Hard cover

Contact:

Ivory Wilson Publisher
A Players' World Enterprises
Ivory Wilson
P.O. Box 70771 Washington, DC 20024
(202) 276-5274
playersworldenterprise@yahoo.com
ISBN0974483001

BOOK REVIEW SLIP

PLAYERS WORLD

Look for the sequel
BIG MACK

ORDER FORM

A players' World Enterprises
Post Office Box 70771
Washington, DC 20024
Phone (202) 276-5274
playersworldenterprise@yahoo.com

Please send me the following book by Ivory Wilson

- ❏ A Players' World $55.00
  Wanna be a pimp
  The manual   Discount: 10%

I understand that I may return any book for a full refund if not satisfied.

Name:_____

Address:_____

_____Zip_____

ISBN0974483001

Shipping $1 for the first book and $.50 for each additional book

A Player's World Enterprises
PO BOX 70771, WASHINGTON, DC 20024, US 12345 (202) 2765274
PLAYERSWORLDENTERPRISES@YAHOO.COM